DINOSAUR BABIES

For a free color catalog describing Gareth Stevens' list of high-quality books and multimedia programs, call 1-800-542-2595 (USA) or 1-800-461-9120 (Canada). Gareth Stevens Publishing's Fax: (414) 225-0377.

Library of Congress Cataloging-in-Publication Data

Green, Tamara, 1945-
  Dinosaur babies/by Tamara Green; illustrated by Richard Grant.
    p. cm. — (World of dinosaurs)
  Includes bibliographical references and index.
  Summary: Discusses young dinosaurs, their hatching,
development, care, and feeding.
  ISBN 0-8368-2290-0 (lib. bdg.)
  1. Dinosaurs—Infancy—Juvenile literature. [1. Dinosaurs.
2. Animals—Infancy.] I. Grant, Richard, 1959- ill. II. Title.
III. Series: World of dinosaurs.
QE862.D5G734826   1999
567.9—dc21   98-48806

This North American edition first published in 1999 by
Gareth Stevens Publishing
1555 North RiverCenter Drive, Suite 201
Milwaukee, Wisconsin 53212 USA

This U.S. edition © 1999 by Gareth Stevens, Inc.
Created with original © 1998 by Quartz Editorial Services,
112 Station Road, Edgware HA8 7AQ U.K.
Additional end matter © 1999 by Gareth Stevens, Inc.

Consultant: Dr. Paul Barrett, Paleontologist, Specialist in Biology and
  Evolution of Dinosaurs, University of Cambridge, England.

Printed in Mexico

1 2 3 4 5 6 7 8 9 03 02 01 00 99

WORLD OF DINOSAURS
DINOSAUR BABIES

by Tamara Green
Illustrated by Richard Grant

Gareth Stevens Publishing
MILWAUKEE

CONTENTS

INTRODUCTION

Fossil evidence provides proof that dinosaurs did not give birth to live young, as mammals do. Instead, as reptilians, they laid fertilized eggs from which their babies would hatch. Fossilized eggs belonging to many species of dinosaurs — among them carnivores like **Troodon** and herbivores like **Protoceratops** and **Hypsilophodon** — have been discovered.

Some eggs seem to have been round in shape; others, however, were more elongated. The eggs varied in size, too. In addition, some clutches of eggs appear to have been laid in spiral formations and others in straight lines or circles, again depending upon the species.

No one has yet come across a **Tyrannosaurus rex** egg. Such a find would be of major scientific importance and worth a small fortune. You may wish to keep your eyes open, since eggs, as well as other dinosaur remains, have been discovered in all sorts of surprising places.

How much do we know about dinosaur babies? What were they like? And how did their parents care for them? Travel with us back in time as we unearth the story of baby dinosaurs — how they were born and how they grew up.

DINOSAUR NESTS

Fossil evidence reveals how some species of dinosaurs prepared for the arrival of the next generation. They prepared nests in which to lay their eggs, and then carefully deposited the eggs in distinctive formations.

The mother **Velociraptor** had recently mated and, not long afterward, began to prepare a nest in which to lay her eggs. First, she deposited several eggs in a hollow dug into the ground. Then she carefully collected dried leaves and other vegetation with which to cover the eggs.

By piling several layers of dried plant material, she would ensure that her eggs were not easily visible to a predator and would, therefore, have the best chance of hatching. The eggs would be kept warm, too, because of this "blanket" covering the nest. As a result, the mother could afford to leave the nest from time to time, although she usually stood guard nearby in order to ward off any approaching enemies.

Paleontologists have discovered that nesting patterns seem to have varied considerably from one species of dinosaur to another. Sauropods, for example, usually laid six to eight eggs at a time, although some may have laid more

and others less, in cases where several mothers shared one nest. These long-necked herbivores arranged the eggs in a circular pattern within the nest, which they probably excavated with their front legs and feet. The large claw on each first digit of some sauropods' forelimbs would have been extremely useful for digging.

Some plant-eaters appear to have laid their eggs in a line, or in two or more parallel rows. Others, such as **Orodromeus**, laid their eggs in a spiral formation — or may have arranged them in this way using their mouths or hands.

Orodromeus — with a name meaning "mountain runner" and found in what is now the state of Montana — were bipedal plant-eaters with horny beaks. When mature, they were about 8 feet (2.4 meters) long. Their nests were circular, for the most part, and measured only about 3 feet (0.9 m) in diameter. Their eggs were laid vertically, with the pointed end facing down.

Some dinosaur eggs, though, seem simply to have been laid at any convenient place on the ground, or in a natural dip or depression.

Annual return

Paleontologists have found traces of two levels of eggs in some sauropod nests — an indication, perhaps, that these mother dinosaurs may have returned to a nesting site to lay eggs there again the following year.

The level at which eggs were deposited may have had a bearing upon temperature level. Some scientists suggest that this, in turn, could have had a direct effect on whether the dinosaur that emerged from the egg was male or female. In any event, there are likely to have been more females born than males. Mature males probably mated with several females each season.

Scientists doubt that huge species of dinosaurs, such as **Tyrannosaurus rex,** would have

laid proportionally larger eggs than smaller species, since there is thought to be a limit to the viable size for an egg. Skeletal remains also show that female dinosaurs had an egg-laying passage with restricted capacity.

7

LOOKING AT DINOSAUR EGGS

Using advanced scanning techniques, scientists have been able to examine the contents of a fossilized dinosaur egg 70 million years or more after it was laid.

The albumen and rich yellow yolk that took up a lot of the space within the tough, oval shell provided the tiny, developing dinosaur embryo with its very own food supply. But even such a natural, well-stocked, built-in larder was not sufficient to ensure survival. The mother had carefully buried her four eggs beneath a pile of rotting vegetation, leaving them to incubate. All would have proceeded normally, but a terrible storm wreaked havoc that day in the prehistoric valley, and the nest was uncovered. The eggs were lightweight and blew away very easily in the strong wind.

As if exposure to such inclement weather was not enough, things soon got even worse. A curious young sauropod made an approach, and, in a playful mood, began to roll one of the eggs down a slope. It promptly hit a rock and the shell cracked open. The baby inside, much too small at this stage to survive without the protection of the eggshell, died within the hour.

Lots of baby dinosaurs probably perished before they were fully developed. There could have been several reasons for their early deaths. Sometimes eggs were victims of climatic conditions, such as floods or high winds. Occasionally, they were damaged as the result of a predator's attack, or their entire contents, embryo and all, may even have been eaten.

Inside story

The illustration shown *at left* demonstrates how some paleontologists believe a dinosaur embryo would have looked when growing inside its shell, if it had been possible to peek inside. No one knows how long it took for a dinosaur egg, such as the one shown here, to hatch.

Experts have suggested that adults may have mated once each year or every other year. Estimates also suggest that a sauropod might easily have laid more than 500 eggs in a 40-year period, although not all would have survived.

In 1955, a team of American paleontologists discovered the fossilized egg of the armored herbivore **Saltasaurus** in Argentina, South America. This egg was 70 million years old and was about half the size of a football and in excellent condition. Anxious to see what might be inside, they used a scanner and found evidence of an embryo at a very early stage of its development.

Examination of other dinosaur eggs has led experts to dismiss the theory that a **Protoceratops** unearthed in Mongolia had died while defending its nest from an **Oviraptor** that was after a nutritious meal. What experts now believe is that the eggs in question were actually those of the **Oviraptor** itself — not those of **Protoceratops**. The so-called "egg-robber" was probably not stealing eggs for its supper after all; instead, it probably died when it became trapped in a sandstorm while defending its own nest. **Oviraptor** had been given the name meaning "egg-robber" because of the early, incorrect interpretation of the circumstances. However, it is still possible that, like some other kinds of dinosaurs, it may have enjoyed a feast of eggs from time to time.

On the surface

Paleontologists have noticed that some dinosaur eggs from the Cretaceous era had ridges and nodules on their shells, whereas those from earlier Triassic and Jurassic times were considerably smoother. The ridges and nodules may have developed to strengthen the shells, but not so greatly that developing babies would have been unable to crack or peck their way out.

NEST-ROBBERS

Some dinosaurs probably found eggs a delicious treat and would go out of their way to raid an obvious nesting site. Other prehistoric creatures may have done the same.

Crunch! A greedy **Troodon**, thought to have been among the most intelligent of all the dinosaurs, quickly grabbed one of the unhatched eggs that lay exposed within the nest. A strong gust of wind had blown away the covering of leaves, and **Troodon** had lost no time in creeping up to the nest, taking advantage of the parent's brief absence as it went off to feed in a nearby copse of trees.

Much of the contents dribbled down **Troodon**'s snout, but it was able to swallow a good deal of the yolk. Soon it would crack open another egg, if there was no sign of the parent's return, and even another, if time allowed.

When you see dinosaur eggs on display in a museum today, they are solid, due to fossilization over millions of years. (These fossilized eggs are known by scientists as ooliths.) Scientists believe that when they were newly laid, however, dinosaur eggs were much more lightweight and fragile.

Easy pickings

Dinosaurs were probably not the only creatures to eat eggs. Just as all sorts of animals — including pigs, hyenas, bears, skunks, snakes, as well as human beings — like to eat eggs today, so a variety of prehistoric creatures may have consumed them at times.

Some types of lizards that exist today were also around in prehistoric times, and some are known egg predators. In fact, they can swallow a chicken's egg whole, crushing it with their throats.

In prehistoric times, some lizards may have tried to eat eggs that were larger than their heads. In such instances, they would not have swallowed them whole, but would have cracked them open instead and eaten their contents.

Mammals from the Mesozoic era were probably too small in general to handle a diet of eggs. Pterosaurs, however, may have been opportunist egg-thieves. What better way to survey a dinosaur nesting site, with the intention of raiding it for eggs, than from the air!

Late Cretaceous **Troodon** has been identified as a likely egg-thief because it had good eyesight. Its hands and feet were also highly suitable for digging and uncovering eggs. **Troodon** remains have been found in ornithopod sites in Montana, suggesting that they died there while attempting to eat eggs or hatchlings.

Experts have even suggested that some egg-thieves may have worked in teams. One or two may have acted as decoys, luring a parent dinosaur away from its nest, so that another could then step in and raid the nest.

VALUABLE FINDS

When were dinosaur eggs first discovered? Where were they found, and by whom? Today, they are highly prized by collectors and sell for large amounts of money at auctions.

The hatchling herbivore, a tiny sauropod, had just emerged from its shell, and it cautiously took a look at the Jurassic world into which it had been born. Soon it would be joined by several siblings, all of which were still inside their eggs. Then their mother could begin to care for her new brood.

The midday sun was scorching, and all traces of dampness on the baby's skin quickly vanished. It would soon be ready for its first meal. It had been very unsteady when it emerged from the egg, but within a few minutes it found its feet and managed to stand. In no time at all, it would be romping, but would keep close to the nest for safety's sake.

Some experts think fossilized dinosaur eggs and small pieces of shell were first discovered many

thousands of years ago, but that those who unearthed them had no idea at all of the sort of creatures to which they had once belonged. In fact, fragments found at a neolithic site in Mongolia suggest they may have been used for primitive forms of jewelry.

Lucky strike

It was not until the nineteenth century, however, that the French Roman Catholic priest Jean-Jacques Pouech, an amateur paleontologist, made a fascinating find. In addition to some

mysterious bones, he unearthed what he described as pieces from enormous eggshells, at least four times the size of ostrich eggs. Their surface, he noticed, was like the skin of an orange, although much harder; and their diameter, he estimated, must have been about 14 inches (35.5 centimeters).

We now know, of course, that what he had found were the remains of dinosaur eggs.

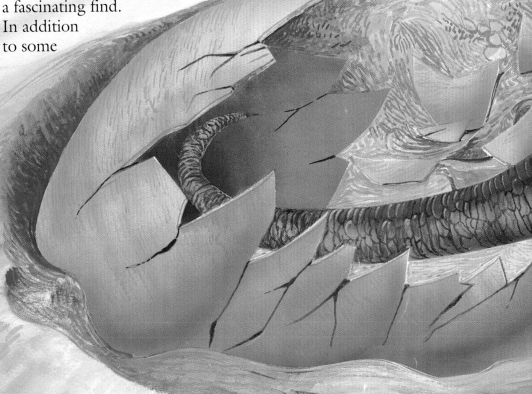

At the time, however, Pouech was uncertain what type of creature had laid the eggs. Over 100 years later, scientists discovered additional pieces of shell only a few hundred yards from the site where the priest had made his interesting discovery.

The region where Pouech made his finds has yielded many fossilized eggs; some have even been discovered by children, entirely by chance. The eggs of sauropods and other plant-eating dinosaurs have since been found in many other parts of the world.

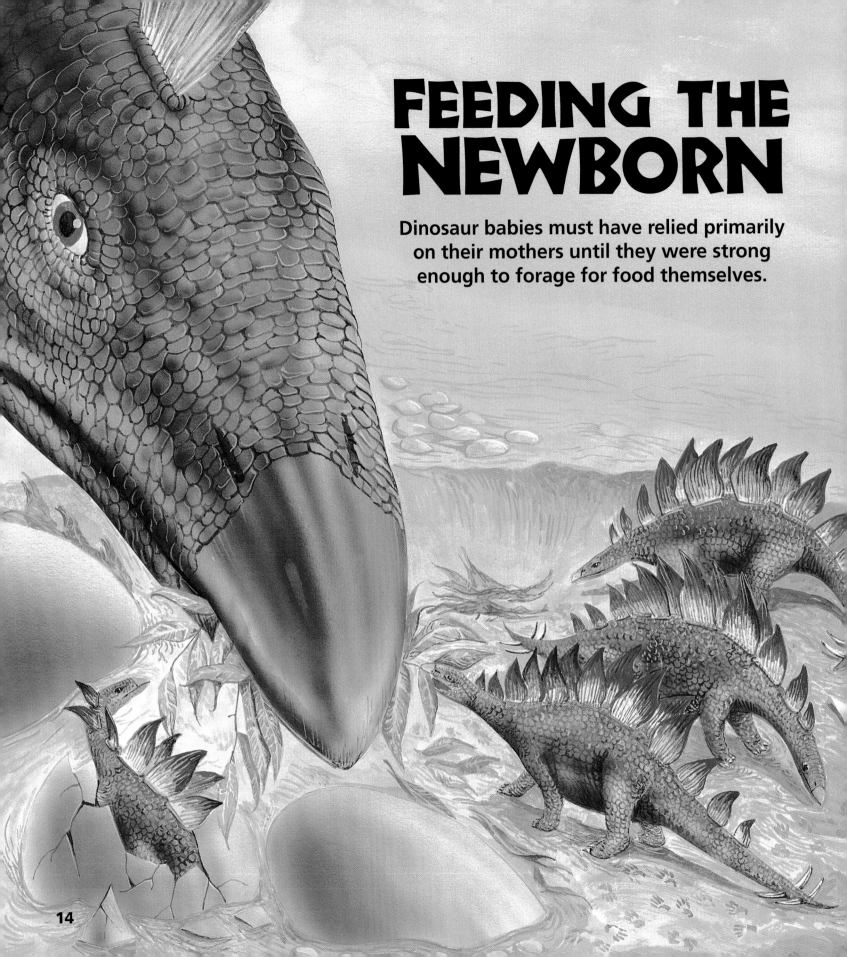

FEEDING THE NEWBORN

Dinosaur babies must have relied primarily on their mothers until they were strong enough to forage for food themselves.

The mother **Stegosaurus** sniffed at the newly hatched babies in her nest, as if to welcome her brood into the Jurassic world. She would, at the same time, get them used to her own body odor, so that the hatchlings would bond with her. They would need to stay close to her for at least several weeks until they learned the art of dinosaur self-sufficiency.

She had already satisfied their hunger by bringing back some crisp vegetation. One or two of the babies gingerly pecked at smaller leaves and tried to swallow them. But the mother knew they would find them indigestible at this young age. She would need to chew the plant material to a pulp herself, then regurgitate it in the form of mush, so that the hatchlings had what amounted to dinosaur baby food.

There was still one egg to hatch, and the emerging baby would be fed in a similar way. The mush probably provided sufficient liquid, too, for the newborn dinosaurs. They were not yet able to travel far in search of food or a water source from which to quench their thirst on a hot Jurassic day. And, if the temperature fell, as it sometimes did, the babies would not suffer as much from the chill if they had been adequately and recently fed.

Rapid growth

Dinosaurs grew at a fantastic rate once they had hatched. It was vital that they were provided with sufficient regular nourishment to ensure rapid growth.

Strong maternal instincts led the mother dinosaurs to feed their babies from the time they were hatched until they were ready to find food on their own. Scientists believe hadrosaur babies, for example, stayed in the nest until their weight increased from under one pound (0.45 kilograms) to about 42 pounds (19 kg), when approximately 8 weeks old. Eventually, some would grow to weigh as much as 2.5 tons — a huge increase in size made over a number of years that, again, could be attributed to good, regular nutritional intake.

Some scientists believe that carnivorous dinosaurs also fed their young regurgitated mush. This meat-eater mush was formed from scraps of raw flesh the parents had obtained by scavenging on remains or killing prey. Unlike human babies, most dinosaurs were probably born with teeth and could therefore chew a little.

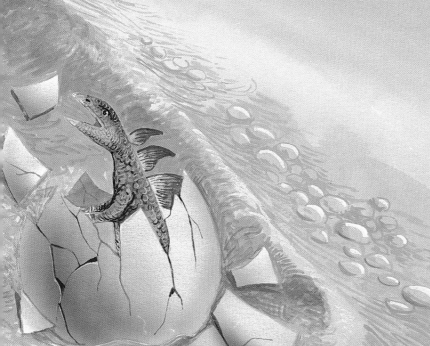

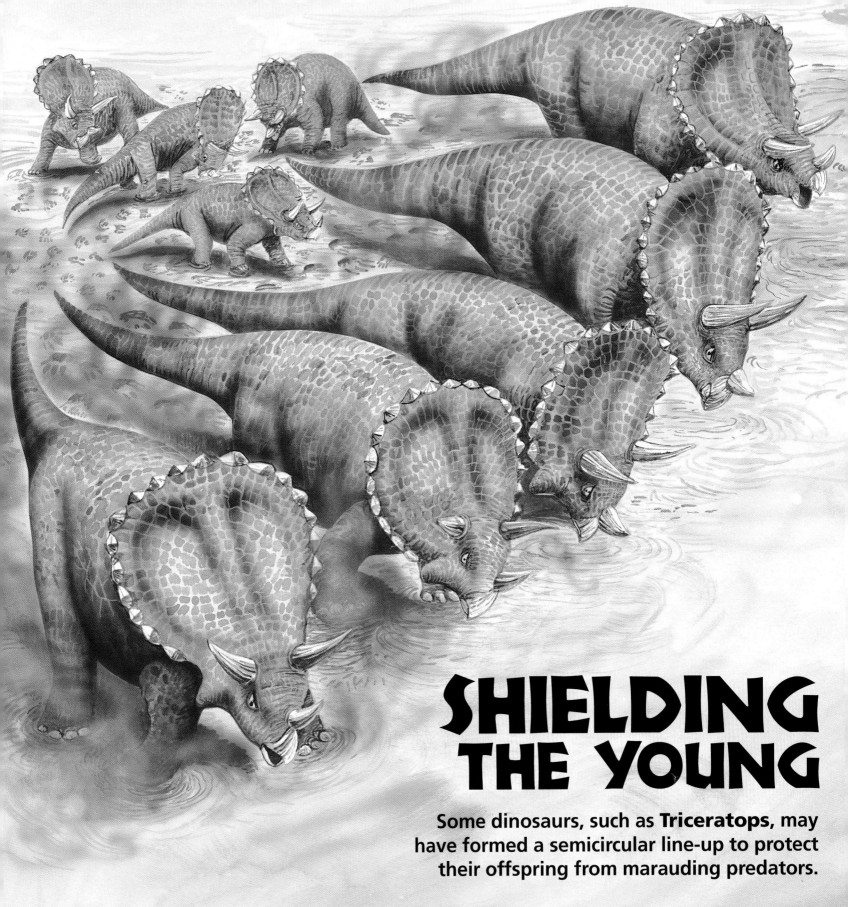

SHIELDING THE YOUNG

Some dinosaurs, such as **Triceratops**, may have formed a semicircular line-up to protect their offspring from marauding predators.

The terrifying roar of a vicious meat-eater took the five adult **Triceratops** entirely by surprise. These horned herbivores had been browsing peacefully on low-lying vegetation, oblivious to the approach of a carnivore that had been stalking them for a long time. It was a very large tyrannosaurid — a close relative of **Tyrannosaurus rex**.

Panic might have set in among the plant-eaters if they had not felt confident enough to engage in a successful counterattack — successful, that is, if they got their timing right.

These three-horned dinosaurs (which is how they came to be named *Triceratops*) were built to offer resistance and could charge an enemy if threatened. Often, they would succeed in knocking an enemy over onto its side, so that it would be able to rise to its feet again only with great difficulty. Meanwhile, the **Triceratops** could make a careful getaway and avoid further confrontation.

As usual, the herbivores had been grazing in the company of several of their young. The one-year-old dinosaurs, already a good size, still needed help from their elders. The adults guided them to the best feeding grounds and protected the more vulnerable young from predators.

Defense strategy

When a hungry meat-eater was on the prowl, a highly effective defense strategy was necessary. Instinctively, the five adult **Triceratops** knew what to do. Leaving their young blissfully unaware of what was going on, they lined up side by side to form a semicircle. With their heads down and magnificent neck frills raised, their bodies formed a living wall between the youngsters and the hungry tyrannosaurid. If it dared to attack for a meal of tender young **Triceratops** flesh, it would first have to contend with five bulky, 30-foot (9-m)-long, 6-ton ceratopsids.

Safety first

The safety of the youngest in the herd was probably always most important when a marauding meat-eater threatened. Several adult dinosaurs probably shared the all-important task of guarding the growing offspring, giving them the best chance possible of reaching adulthood without falling victim to hungry and fearsome attackers.

Some dinosaurs might have protected their young in other ways, however. A large carnivore, for instance, probably only needed to rely on its very presence to deter a potential predator from going for its young. Others may have roared very loudly to scare an enemy, or reared up, threatening to retaliate. On occasions, too, maybe a whole group used combined force. Survival of the next generation was of vital importance.

SUPER-MOMS

When paleontologists discovered a dinosaur that obviously tended to its young until they were able to be fully independent, the scientists gave it a name meaning "good mother lizard."

Several hadrosaur mothers stood alongside their nests, surveying activity in the area. Within the hollowed-out nests, the young duck-bills chirped loudly, signaling their emergence into the Cretaceous world. A faint cheeping could even be heard from inside eggs that had not yet hatched, but were nearly ready to crack open.

This nesting area, in what is now western North America, resembled a dinosaur nursery. It made sense for the females to nest in a colony, where there was safety in numbers. Predators would be less likely to attack if there were lots of large, devoted mothers to ward them off. Also, other mothers could guard the nest if one went off to find food for her young.

It was in 1978 that the American paleontologists Jack Horner and Robert Makela decided to visit a fossil shop in Montana. While viewing the many items on display, the scientists noticed the bones of what appeared to be a baby hadrosaur.

The paleontologists were very curious as to where the bones had been unearthed. After inquiring about the location, they decided to visit it for themselves. What they discovered that day is now acknowledged as one of the most remarkable dinosaur finds ever.

Long-term care

It had always been assumed that dinosaurs, like many reptiles of today, abandoned their young after birth, leaving them to fend for themselves. Now it seemed that this theory was about to be turned on its head. In fact, there was evidence to show that these hadrosaur babies had stayed in the nests for a considerable time, crushing the remains of their shells as they moved around in the bowl-shaped hollows. Their mothers must have continued to care for them during this time. Therefore, this particular species of hadrosaur was given the name *Maiasaura*, meaning "good mother lizard."

Eventually, Horner and Makela and their colleagues found fourteen nests, thirty-one babies, and forty-two eggs at the site. Then, in 1984, Horner found a bone bed where about ten thousand **Maiasaura** had met their deaths, most probably as the result of a volcanic eruption. Nesting grounds located in the region extended to about 2 miles (3.2 kilometers) in length. Among the dinosaurs living at this site would have been many babies and juveniles of various ages and sizes. But when such a catastrophe occurred, even such "super-moms" as **Maiasaura** could do nothing to save their offspring.

TINIEST SKELETONS

Certain skeletal remains show that some baby dinosaurs were probably very small when they first hatched out of their prehistoric eggs.

The intense midday sun had finally dried up the last of the remaining puddles, revealing several small skeletons exposed on the ground. They lay side by side, with no trace of flesh remaining. Their presence occasionally attracted the curiosity of a prehistoric lizard or insect, such as the large, colorful Triassic dragonfly that had just landed.

Death for these dinosaur hatchlings had come much too soon, the result of a flash flood that had washed them away from the safety of their nest, along with fragments of the shells from which they had only recently emerged. Their mother had died, too, in the torrent. Soon their delicate bones would be completely covered by the shifting sands — although not to be lost forever.

Some 220 million years later, in 1979, a team of paleontologists led by José F. Bonaparte and M. Vince unearthed the remains of these very same babies in a region of what is now Patagonia, in Argentina, South America. They were very well preserved and, so far, date among the tiniest baby dinosaurs ever found. They were probably siblings from a single clutch of eggs.

The scenario of their death, as described here, is a likely one. But the babies might have perished as the result of some sort of disease, or extremes of temperature that they could not tolerate, or attack by a predator — although it is doubtful that the skeletons would have remained whole if the hatchlings had been savaged.

A modest start

Not all dinosaurs were huge, of course, like the giant long-necks or fearsome carnivores. Some, such as **Compsognathus**, were as small as a turkey, even when fully grown. And it seems, from the remains discovered of a baby **Mussaurus,** that even species of dinosaurs that grew to substantial proportions may have been very small when they started out in life.

Mussaurus measured about 10 feet (3 m) from the tip of its snout to the end of its tail when mature. When young, however, as each skeleton found in Argentina shows, its body was a mere 12 inches (30 cm) long, with a skull so tiny that it was only 1 inch (2.5 cm) in length. The remains of each baby **Mussaurus** are small enough to fit in the palms of an adult human's hands.

Mussaurus clearly had a lot of growing to do before it reached its full adult size. In fact, it would have to grow twenty times larger. If you were to grow twenty times your birth size, you would probably end up with a height of about 30 feet (9 m)!

Some scientists have suggested that the skeletal remains of the **Mussaurus** babies may not have been from hatchlings. Instead, these small skeletons may have been from embryos that died as a result of some disaster that struck the eggs while they were still developing inside.

We may never know exactly what happened on that fatal Triassic day. What is certain, however, is that it is highly unusual for such small and fragile bones to remain relatively intact over many millions of years.

Mussaurus was a prosauropod that roamed the globe's one great landmass, known as Pangaea, during Triassic times. North America and South America had not yet broken off from this vast prehistoric continent. It is possible that other remains of this dinosaur may one day be discovered — perhaps including more skeletons of babies or infants. From the remains found so far, paleontologists can only speculate how **Mussaurus** looked as a newly hatched dinosaur, and as a significantly larger adult.

CANNIBALS!

Strange as it may seem, paleontologists have found evidence that some dinosaurs resorted to eating their own young at times, perhaps during extreme stress.

A terrible squealing echoed through the arid Triassic valley, in what is now the state of New Mexico. The noise was extremely high-pitched, and clearly served as a distress signal of some kind. It was accompanied by a furious scurrying, as a group of terrified baby dinosaurs attempted to escape from their nest.

It had been only four days since these hatchling **Coelophysis** had emerged from their eggs. Under normal circumstances, these slim, pack-hunting carnivores would grow to be about 10 feet (3 m) in length and 65 pounds (29.5 kg) in weight. The lives of these babies, however, were to be cut short in a very dramatic way.

At first, the juveniles had relied entirely on their mother, who brought them partially digested scraps of food to eat. On this particular day, however, several adult dinosaurs of their species, including the babies' mother, had violently turned on them.

As if suffering from dementia of some kind, the adults began to grab at the babies before, quite literally, making a meal of them.

The adult **Coelophysis** had suddenly become cannibalistic!

Baby skeletons

David Baldwin, a nineteenth-century American scientist, first discovered the 210-million-year-old remains of the dinosaur **Coelophysis** in New Mexico in 1881. He was a fossil-hunter for Edward Drinker Cope, who gave this dinosaur its name meaning "hollow bones." Baldwin found the incomplete skeletons of three dinosaurs of different sizes, which were identified as **Coelophysis** of different ages. Over 60 years later, in 1947, a team from New York's American Museum of Natural History revisited the site. These scientists felt confident that there might be more bones to be unearthed.

As they had anticipated, the paleontologists found many partial skeletons — but they were also in for a big surprise. To their great amazement, they found the bones of a number of **Coelophysis** babies inside the rib cages of some of the adults of their species. At first, the scientists wondered whether these infants could have been developing inside their mothers' bodies when the adults perished millions of years ago. However, this explanation was soon rejected since it was already common knowledge that dinosaurs laid eggs instead of giving birth to live young. What, then, could have happened to make the parent dinosaurs swallow these infants whole?

Experts are not sure, but they can make an intelligent guess based on their knowledge of other animals. In modern times, some carnivorous mammals — such as lions and bears — become cannibalistic if they are under extreme stress, perhaps if no other food is available or if the adult males want to eliminate the offspring of rival males.

Whatever the circumstances with **Coelophysis**, some disaster must have followed soon after. The remains showed that the adult **Coelophysis** did not have time to digest their intake before they themselves died.

JOINING THE HERD

Fossilized tracks seem to indicate baby dinosaurs did not wander far from the nest until they had grown to at least four times their birth size.

The tropical storm gradually abated, having refreshed the arid Jurassic landscape in what is now China. Three baby **Oshanosaurus** continued to take shelter under their mother's towering body. The young sauropods were enjoying a game of dinosaur hide-and-seek as they scampered between her pillarlike legs. She would have to be careful to avoid crushing them underfoot when they played beneath her in this carefree way.

During the many weeks that the hatchlings were confined to the nest, the mother sauropod had taken very good care of her offspring. Eventually, they would learn to feed themselves.

Like all young dinosaurs, they had fewer teeth than an adult. They did not need a full set of teeth at this early age since they would at first eat only soft leaves and vegetation. Later, when their diet became more varied and substantial, they would mimic the adults and swallow small stones, known as gastroliths, to help grind tougher vegetation and aid digestion. Soon it would be time for these babies to join the rest of the herd as they foraged for food.

Fossilized footprints

Only a few remains of baby dinosaurs have been found throughout the world. This is probably because the infants' more fragile bones broke up and disintegrated more easily over the millions of years since the time of dinosaurs. Some bones of juvenile dinosaurs have been found in places as far apart as China, India, Argentina, Canada, and the United States.

Scientists have also been able to learn more about dinosaur babies by studying their fossilized footprints. These trace fossils reveal that when a sauropod herd traveled to find fresh feeding grounds, the young were sheltered in the center of the group. In this way, the more vulnerable infants were protected by all the adults, and not just their mothers. This behavior also kept the young dinosaurs from wandering off or getting left behind.

Some paleontologists have suggested that the young of some species of dinosaurs had different coloring from their parents, providing camouflage as the juveniles moved through the vegetation. This protective coloration would have been especially helpful for species that did not live as a herd. The young, therefore, could not benefit from the protection that communal living had to offer.

Since no proof exists as to the color of a dinosaur's skin, experts have had to make intelligent guesses when creating museum displays or illustrating books. Most dinosaurs are pictured as having coloration somewhat similar to modern reptiles.

YOUNG CARNIVORES

**Were baby meat-eating dinosaurs independent right from birth?
Or did they need their mother's care, just like an herbivore baby,
if they were to survive the rigors of the prehistoric world?**

The larger juvenile **Segnosaurus** was excited after spotting a large termite nest under construction. The dinosaur immediately began to poke into the nest with its narrow toothless beak and the three sharply clawed fingers on each hand. The insects would provide a good source of nourishment for the young bipedal theropod. Its fast-growing but smaller sibling would soon learn to make the most of such a nutritious meal by mimicking this attack on the nest.

Later, the pair could fish and look for other creatures on which to prey. The older **Segnosaurus** had often watched its mother hunt for food and was now old enough to be on its own — unless a much larger and hungry meat-eater was on the lookout for a meal and threatened to pounce.

So far, no one has found the remains of a young **Segnosaurus**, so we can only guess what they looked like and how they spent their days. In fact, very few theropod eggs or juvenile theropod skeletons of any species have been unearthed — only fragments of young **Syntarsus**, **Coelophysis**, **Allosaurus**, **Tyrannosaurus rex**, **Troodon**, **Tarbosaurus**, and **Gallimimus** skeletons. Experts have had to make very general assumptions about a carnivore's early years, and at times they have had very different opinions.

Varying views

Many scientists think that the majority of meat-eaters probably looked after their young and fed them until they were about half-grown. Others, however, think it is likely that young theropods were left on their own shortly after birth. These experts point out that dinosaurs and birds are now thought to be related. Some species of birds, they note, build a nest for their young, thereby ensuring that the eggs remain at a suitable temperature. Once the young hatch, however, the parents immediately abandon the babies. Cuckoos do not even make a nest for their eggs, but deposit them instead in the nests of other birds. Is it possible that theropod dinosaurs exhibited the same types of behavior? The question remains unanswered.

There is also debate within the scientific community about how long it took theropods to reach maturity. Some experts believe that huge

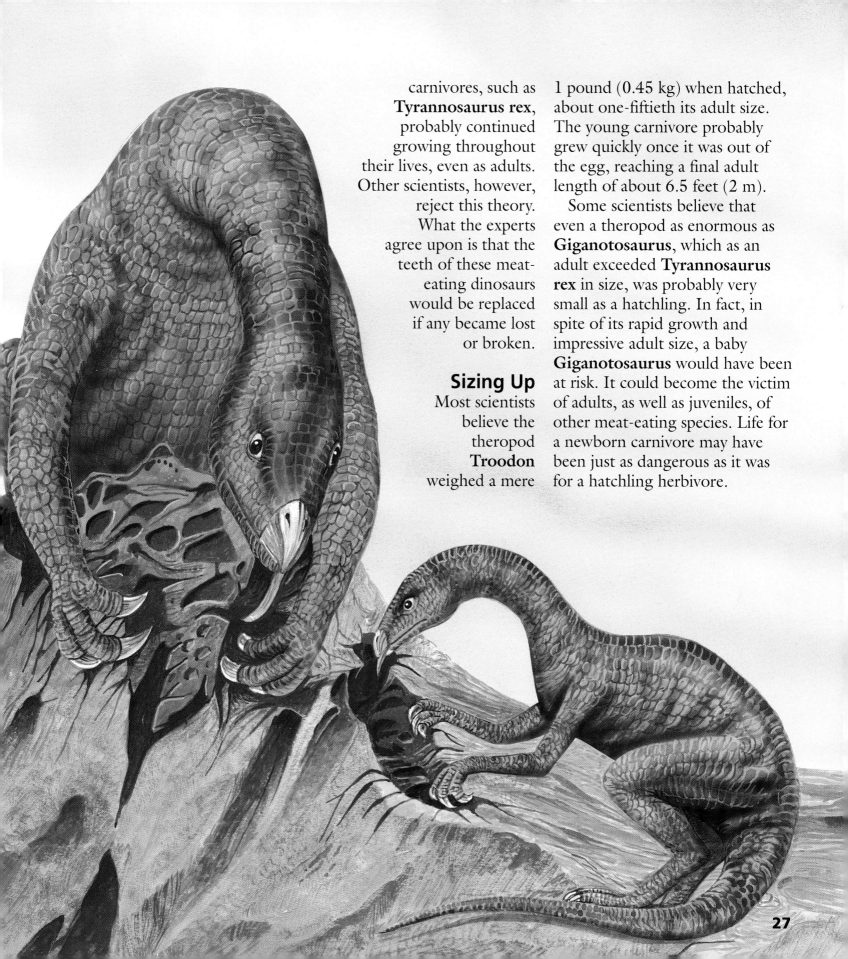

carnivores, such as **Tyrannosaurus rex**, probably continued growing throughout their lives, even as adults. Other scientists, however, reject this theory. What the experts agree upon is that the teeth of these meat-eating dinosaurs would be replaced if any became lost or broken.

Sizing Up

Most scientists believe the theropod **Troodon** weighed a mere 1 pound (0.45 kg) when hatched, about one-fiftieth its adult size. The young carnivore probably grew quickly once it was out of the egg, reaching a final adult length of about 6.5 feet (2 m).

Some scientists believe that even a theropod as enormous as **Giganotosaurus**, which as an adult exceeded **Tyrannosaurus rex** in size, was probably very small as a hatchling. In fact, in spite of its rapid growth and impressive adult size, a baby **Giganotosaurus** would have been at risk. It could become the victim of adults, as well as juveniles, of other meat-eating species. Life for a newborn carnivore may have been just as dangerous as it was for a hatchling herbivore.

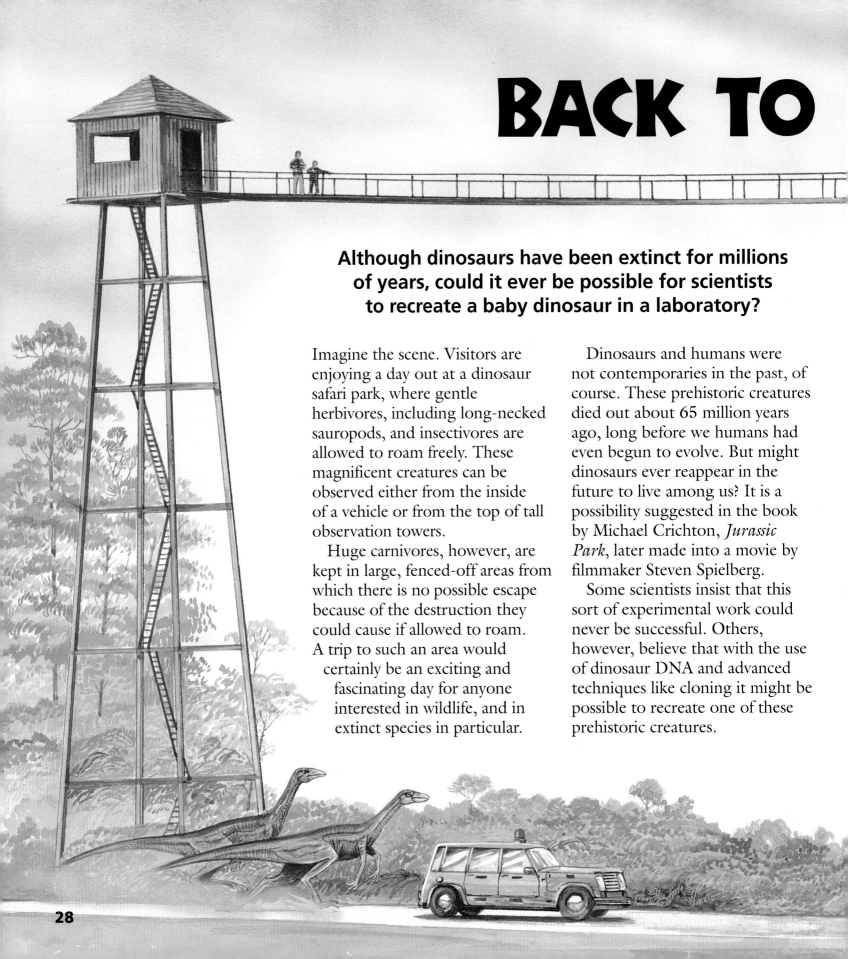

BACK TO

Although dinosaurs have been extinct for millions of years, could it ever be possible for scientists to recreate a baby dinosaur in a laboratory?

Imagine the scene. Visitors are enjoying a day out at a dinosaur safari park, where gentle herbivores, including long-necked sauropods, and insectivores are allowed to roam freely. These magnificent creatures can be observed either from the inside of a vehicle or from the top of tall observation towers.

Huge carnivores, however, are kept in large, fenced-off areas from which there is no possible escape because of the destruction they could cause if allowed to roam. A trip to such an area would certainly be an exciting and fascinating day for anyone interested in wildlife, and in extinct species in particular.

Dinosaurs and humans were not contemporaries in the past, of course. These prehistoric creatures died out about 65 million years ago, long before we humans had even begun to evolve. But might dinosaurs ever reappear in the future to live among us? It is a possibility suggested in the book by Michael Crichton, *Jurassic Park*, later made into a movie by filmmaker Steven Spielberg.

Some scientists insist that this sort of experimental work could never be successful. Others, however, believe that with the use of dinosaur DNA and advanced techniques like cloning it might be possible to recreate one of these prehistoric creatures.

THE FUTURE

DNA (deoxyribonucleic acid) is the main constituent of chromosomes and is responsible for all hereditary characteristics. It is what makes a baby elephant, for example, have characteristics similar to its parents. If, as some scientists suggest, we could get hold of some dinosaur DNA, we might somehow and sometime be able to "make" a dinosaur.

In *Jurassic Park*, scientists succeed in obtaining dinosaur DNA from an insect. It had once bitten a dinosaur, taking in some of its blood. Later, the insect became trapped and fossilized in tree resin, known as amber.

Author Crichton's book also suggests that it could be possible to recreate a dinosaur by cloning, if you could find one that had not been fossilized but, instead, had been preserved in a peat bog, frozen solid, or mummified.

If scientists used the DNA extraction technique, they might not be able to tell initially which species of dinosaur they were about to recreate. It might later be possible, as described in *Jurassic Park*, to ensure that all resulting babies were female by controlling the environment of the eggs. In the book, this was done to prevent the recreated dinosaurs from mating naturally when they grew to maturity, so that the population would be kept under control.

Who knows if one day this science fiction could become science for real!

GLOSSARY

albumen — the white of an egg.

amber — a brownish-yellow material that is the hardened resin of prehistoric pine trees.

bipedal — relating to an animal that walks or moves on two feet.

ceratopsids — members of a group of dinosaurs with horns and frills, such as Triceratops.

chromosome — the cell nucleus or microscopic body that contains DNA. The genes that pass on hereditary characteristics are made up of chromosomes.

cloning — creating a genetically identical creature from a single existing one.

clutch (n) — a nest of eggs; a brood, or group, of young animals hatched from eggs.

communal — relating to a community of animals or plants; shared or used in common.

contemporaries — individuals living at the same time.

Cretaceous times — the final era of the dinosaurs, lasting from 144-65 million years ago.

DNA — a substance in animal and plant chromosomes that is responsible for hereditary characteristics, such as eye color.

embryo — an animal in the first stage of development before birth.

evolve — to adapt and change over a period of time to suit changing environments.

forage — to wander in search of food for grazing or browsing.

gastroliths — small stones swallowed by certain plant-eating dinosaurs to help digest tough plant material.

hadrosaur — a member of a group of duck-billed dinosaurs.

hereditary — transmitted by genes and DNA from parent to offspring.

instincts — ways of behaving that are natural, or automatic, rather than learned.

Jurassic times — the middle era of the dinosaurs, lasting from 213-144 million years ago.

Mesozoic — the long period of time during which the dinosaurs lived, divided into the Triassic, Jurassic, and Cretaceous eras.

mimic — to copy or imitate someone or something.

neolithic — relating to an earlier age or period of time, such as the Stone Age.

offspring — the young of an animal or plant.

ooliths — fossilized eggs.

paleontologist — a scientist who studies past geologic periods as they are known from fossils.

primitive — in an early stage of development; not highly developed or evolved.

prosauropod — any member of a group of moderately long-necked dinosaurs, all herbivores, mainly from Triassic times.

sauropod — a member of a group of long-necked, plant-eating dinosaurs, mainly from Jurassic times, which had small heads and five-toed feet.

siblings — one of two or more individuals having the same parent; a brother or sister.

stalking — following prey in a slow and secretive way; going through an area in this manner looking for prey.

theropods — members of a group of meat-eating bipedal dinosaurs.

Triassic times — the first era of the dinosaurs, lasting from 249-213 million years ago.

viable — able to survive; able to grow and develop.

MORE BOOKS TO READ

Baby Dinosaur. Peter Dodson (Scholastic)

Dinosaur Babies. Ely Kish
  (National Geographic Society)

Dinosaur Babies. Lucille Recht Penner
  (Random House)

Dinosaur Babies. Maida Silverman
  (Simon & Schuster Books for Young Readers)

The Dinosaur Egg Mystery. M. Christina Butler
  (Barron's Educational Series)

Dinosaurs. David Norman (Knopf)

Dinosaurs and How They Lived. Steve Parker
  (Dorling Kindersley)

Discovering Dinosaur Babies. Miriam Schlein
  (Four Winds Press)

A Family of Dinosaurs. Mary Le Duc O'Neill
  (Troll Associates)

How Did Dinosaurs Live? Kunihiko Hisa (Lerner)

The New Dinosaur Collection (series).
  (Gareth Stevens)

World of Dinosaurs (series). (Gareth Stevens)

VIDEOS

All About Dinosaurs. (United Learning)

Dinosaur! (series). (Arts & Entertainment Network)

Dinosaurs. (DeBeck Educational Video)

Dinosaurs. (Smithsonian Video)

Dinosaurs. (Walt Disney Home Video)

Dinosaurs, Dinosaurs, Dinosaurs.
  (Twin Tower Enterprises)

Learning About Dinosaurs. (Trans-Atlantic Video)

WEB SITES

www.clpgh.org/cmnh/discovery/

www.dinodon.com/index.html

www.dinosauria.com/

www.dinosociety.org/

www.nationalgeographic.com/Features/96/dinoeggs/

www.ZoomDinosaurs.com

Due to the dynamic nature of the Internet, some web sites stay current longer than others. To find additional web sites, use a reliable search engine with one or more of the following keywords to help you locate more information about dinosaurs. Keywords: *dinosaurs, DNA, fossils, paleontology, prehistoric.*

INDEX